Free Verse Editions
Edited by Jon Thompson

This History That Just Happened

Hannah Craig

Winner of the New Measure Poetry Prize

Parlor Press
Anderson, South Carolina
www.parlorpress.com

Parlor Press LLC, Anderson, South Carolina, 29621

Library of Congress Cataloging-in-Publication Data

Names: Craig, Hannah, author.
Title: This history that just happened / Hannah Craig.
Description: Anderson, South Carolina : Parlor Press, [2017] |
Series: Free verse editions | "Winner of the New Measure Poetry
Prize."
Identifiers: LCCN 2017038921 | ISBN 9781602359024 (pbk. :
alk. paper)
Classification: LCC PS3603.R3534 A6 2017 | DDC 811/.6--
dc23
LC record available at https://lccn.loc.gov/2017038921

978-1-60235-902-4 (paperback)
978-1-60235-903-1 (PDF)
978-1-60235-904-8 (epub)

2 3 4 5

Cover design by David Blakesley.
Cover image: "LightBoxPaper92" © Jean A. Kirby. Used by
    permission.
Printed on acid-free paper.

Parlor Press, LLC is an independent publisher of scholarly and
trade titles in print and multimedia formats. This book is available
in paperback and ebook formats from Parlor Press on the World
Wide Web at http://www.parlorpress.com or through online and
brick-and-mortar bookstores. For submission information or to
find out about Parlor Press publications, write to Parlor Press,
3015 Brackenberry Drive, Anderson, South Carolina, 29621, or
email editor@parlorpress.com.

Contents

Acknowledgments   vii

I   1

Faith Healing   3
Natti Crow Road   4
The Horses   5
You Know I'm Right to Do So   6
The Dream-Want   7
The Little Sleep   9
White-Footed Bird   11
In Which You Are Disappearing from the
Natural World Obviously   12
Institution Pool   13
And There, That Was the Middle   14
O It Rises   15
Everything Sends   16
Referential   17
It May Taste Sweet   18
Grandmother   19
Beach House   20
Spring Cleaning   21
From the Reformed Presbyterian Theological
Seminary on the First Warm Day in March, a
Man Comes Running in a White T-Shirt   22
Teaching Me to Shoot   23
Returned   24
April Snow   25
Turkish March   26
Amsterdam   27

Contents

II 29

Pain Questionnaire 31
Pain Has No Future but Itself 32
Cuticle 34
From One Thing, Another 35
The Scalded Map 36
Job 37
Translation 38
Snare 40
Fever 41
White Powder 43
Poinsettia 45

III 47

Flora – Winter 49
Flora — Spring 52
Flora — Summer 55
Flora — Autumn 58
Teleology of the Atl-Atl 60
Teleology of Dark Fibre 61
Teleology of Febreze 64
Teleology of the Clock 66
Lawrenceville 68
Moss I 69
Moss II 70

Free Verse Editions 73
About the Author 75

Acknowledgments

I wish to gratefully acknowledge the following journals where several of these poems made their first appearances: Copper Nickel, Emrys, Hampden-Sydney Review, Handsome, Mid-American Review, Mississippi Review, North American Review, Prairie Schooner, Salamander, and Third Wednesday.

My sincere gratitude and admiration go out to Yusef Komunyakaa, Jon Thompson, David Blakesley, and all at Parlor Press who made this book happen.

Thanks to Ash Bowen, Richard Epstein, Nevid Hartenstein, Steve Mueske, and William Neumire for being my poetry community for so long! And thanks to Jean Kirby for the all the art!

My unending love and thanks to Matthew, Mara, Rebekah, Mary, Sarah, Martha, Elia, Christopher, and Brandon.

I

Faith Healing

It's early January in northeastern Indiana, crows
on the roof ridge of the barn. Just beyond the house,
a row of maples, sap humming, not yet bullfrogged
into full song, just athump, thump, thump,
in those stiff, dark bodies.

Turns out the power to heal is as transgressive as the power
to open jar lids. Warm-water tricks, counter taps
can't loose anything at all. Just so much numb calculation,
hauled up against windbreak cladding.

A lonely gunshot, halting glossy green flight, challenges law
with every distraught call. For you have been redeemed
faster than the night-clam, pearly jaw hinged
by star-teeth. Faster than fever taking the roads
one by one, until they glisten, all mute black-ice.
Faster than the skin's change, fingerling cracks
in the frail earth.

The midwife, plunging her hands into the sink,
finds she cannot feel any of her fingers, cannot sense
the expected apparition. Only the talons
of an owl on her shoulder, a realization
that preparation is insufficient, that tools are
insignificant. There must be insurance, there must be
a network of accountability.

Instead, only bloodscent in the anteroom,
pipes frozen shut, green apple wood burning,
icicles like a dumb drumline—dripping their tat-a-tat-tat.
White fields meeting white sky, meeting the strangely-returned eye
which has come to mourn its parentage, its history,
to ask for holiness, find none.

Natti Crow Road

That day when he came in he said. *Look honey, I have some bad news.* And the electricity had been shut off, which I found hard to believe, so I sped through the house throwing on the switches and nothing, nothing. Asking what happened, what happened to all the money? *Please stop please, you'll make me throw my back out* he said, holding my elbow, his thumb digging into the tender place, but not unkindly, more like beseeching. And already the heat from the afternoon was creeping, damp and heavy, under the screen door and into the kitchen. I wanted to put the kids in the bathtub to cool down but the well was electric, too, so we just sat on the lawn eating green grapes and singing songs. But look it was worth the knots, the braille written into hot bodies, freckles, scars, stretch marks. The girls lying on the blanket in the grass, their honey curls and honey breath. *This is how it was a long time ago,* he said. But there's nothing the same, really. Next door the neighbor's air conditioning unit sung and hummed, kicking on and off and on. But this is much harder than it sounds, because in the dark we wanted desire to make a mark, to spark, to let something fly, to jerk. For this to be the reverie of summer, a back porch cooling, there had to be contrast and release, darkness abbreviated, bounded by lights, and cool air hitting the heat, building a lattice of fog-work and confusion on which the white aphelion unfurls. Born of air we were, but pressed. On a slightly related note, a fire engine, solo across the country, probably too late, too late, but still calling.

The Horses

Back then snow would erase all
but gray roads shearing away
at stippled fields. On cold days,
the horses would stand
near the south wall of the stable,
their forelegs sheathed
in mud. There was a walnut tree
grew there, interlocked knuckles
skidding across the snowy paddock.

And those days, riding with Regina
in her troubled Honda, having just come
from the warm houses of our mothers,
we'd prepare ourselves for the horses,
winter growth of manes and tails,
fuzz and furr, by winding up
a throwing arm. Aloft the half-bit

breakfast apple, for a moment,
like some fat-bottomed bird,
a spit red jewel in its set
of so much snow. The knobs
caught in our throats, the fabula
of mildewed kitchens,
vengeful mamas.

Regina, wet-haired, glossy, tough,
would push a tape into the deck,
Snoop Dogg, let's say, and some
swift curse would seem
to set the scene. Bitch please.
I gives a fuck.
Or that one perfectly knowable refrain—
I never a met a girl that I love
in the whole wide world.[1]

1. Lyrics in "The Horses" are from Snoop Dogg's "Ain't No Fun (If the Homies Can't Have None)."

You Know I'm Right to Do So

This week I realized that I'd forgotten the names of everyone
I ever knew who made meth. *Cooked* it, like it was a curry.

Like it was a broth or marrow. I forgot their names and what
I was doing with them, those chemists in plaid shirts and jeans.

I forgot their names and their quiet dissipation, how they went
from bodies into shadows and from there, into chairs

in the cooling university courtyard where I had gone to live.
This was already between us and changing everything.

I forgot that saying goodbye seemed for sure like the last time and
    was.
O I was vicious with all that indifference and felt it. And now I
    forget

How it feels to turn out of the Enchanted Hills trailer park
onto the county road. The negative space of a trillion uncounted

organisms, riding the rods of heat and light, spitting out electrons
with amazing fury. And the pickling smell on worn flannel, the
    odor

of adhesion and dilution. The hairline fracture between
car window and nightlight, into which our breath

would go, carrying out all its dire smoke. And now,
to use them, the makers of meth, the Indiana boys,

the kings of hard-science that I could not fathom. To use them
after having bested them. And still, somehow, to lose them.

The Dream-Want

Among the Iroquois a person recovering from a long illness will often say *I nearly ate strawberries, I nearly drank their juice.*

A person who doesn't recover says nothing at all.

The thing with faith-healing is that, by the time you know, it's too late. It helps now that I think of all that time as a dream. It helps when I think of the deep red strawberry juice in white porcelain cups.

Of us all sitting around sipping it.

The thing you wanted in your dream was a holiness around you, a white heat around you. Which meant we could make it so. We could keep it so by not saying a word in the house.

By not saying a word in the car.

My sword and shield, you always said.

You died because you went off your insulin. How's that for first impressions?

What lives is the manner of all our love, the wet boards and pipes, the burst wood. The church, uneven and stinking. The silver folding chairs, arranged in equal rows. A kitchen table in the dark house where you sat with your hands on your face, weeping for the uneven blessings, for the inequality of the blessings.

Because it is written, be ye holy for I am holy.

The thing with faith-healing is the dream gets the better of you.

That midnight when the baby was still small, she had a fever so high that I could feel the heat a foot away. I got into the bath holding her. I put my hands on the flushed skin of her back and thought if I could have faith in something, I would have faith in the water, I would have so much faith in the water.

My husband came in with the medicine in its red bottle. He said there's always the Urgent Care, if we need it.

When I think of you, you are lying on a mattress, on the floor. Your hand is on your face, covering it. Your guitar strap is around your chest, but I do not see the guitar anywhere.

There should be music that now must all be unwritten.

Remember when the Amish boy was dying in the road and you ran out, pleading the blood? Nobody else in the world will know what I mean. But the way you held him in the pink blanket, I thought you could do it, I thought for sure you were going to really do it.

The changing of our mortal bodies, you wrote.

And if it went through you like that, the light, the light, if it half-blinded you so you stumbled in the gravel of the driveway, put your hand out and touched the peach tree, which, just then, was hanging with ripe fruit, well, it was not your fault that you seemed so powerful, that you held so much vigor, so much red, sweet heat in your blood.

The Little Sleep

Think of death, think of driving
through the game preserve on rain
& brake fluid,
between Shock Lake and Bass Pond
gravel & dirt & rich blood
 deer strung in oak trees
hunt caps in the orange trees slow-walking
thighs like cold barrels
rolling, rolling

Look, the dialogue of new death
is broader, forget what you heard on Sunday,
this is new speech
floating across the yard, someone's forearm
braced against the bedroom window,
a tin-lip shaped on milk glass
a forethought in chipped polish

Shoot a memento, subsistence or justice.
Shoot back-talkers, antlers, tigers, kids.

Suddenly there's so much churl in the fanning swamp-water.
So much curl in the fern leaves where the frost drops
like duck eggs.

Three languages now, instead of one.
Two of these show that the powerful need to eat first.
They must or they die, I think.

That's why the birds kettle
to a big bass drum on Indiana evenings,
boom-tock-boom.
The fox scrambles to the ditch
but we keep thinking of measurements:
number of eggs for custard
number of eggs for a silky afternoon

number of softened, soaked vanilla beans
the powerful need to serve a sit-down meal
roast, bread, beans
the coroner's gray sedan
wheels of needling silence, rims of ice
and the cows with their muddy boots

the farmer brings out the eggs on his carbon-fiber leg
he used to shoot Afghans, now shoos chickens
& ducks aside   come on so come on

an egg dark as brass, some jam
again the ferny green that never truly evaporates
from the rims and fallen limbs along the bank
like the green trim on this flat sheet
fails to offer comfort or much dignity
anyway, warriors, the light here now
the light of how committed we have become to rigidity

to what is only here this little while
of how we are to nowhere called and to all places bound.

White-Footed Bird

The barns slump into themselves. Dead leaves, damp leaves.
The members of our tribe are bywoners, a gentry of mice

and loose black tea. In the new times of this tribe, the burgeoning
times of this tribe, we have made inroads and alleys, we've lifted

thousands of rocks so that we can cultivate their homes for our own,
so we can search for the rare white-footed bird who loves rocky places.

Our tribe with its narrowing skulls, its senility, its constraints on fuel.
And then the bird is spotted and counted and found to be far more
    populist

than first imagined, indiscriminately sharing nests with barn swallows
or even robins, eating garbage. It's plausible the tribe took a wrong turn,

that there's something we've lost, the ability to truly feel cold,
the inability to waltz, a failure of articulation. It doesn't seem to matter,

now, where we've been, the dark ink of midnights,
the fragility of scrub oaks, the flannel sheets. It's the first time we've ever
    heard it,

the mournful call of the bird, that bird, a ghost in the throat of the bird,
a wound windrel, a timid clock ticking, faintly, flicking its wings back, back

to sleep, to wake, to sleep. Wait, wait.
We're a lost tribe, a wood violet following another wood violet,

a woman who turns back to look behind
and says slow down slow down.

Ankle-deep in the creek bed, we've come to terms
with the icy slaloms of moss and water,

the weird little phantasms of mud-colored fish,
the white bird who fishes there, the thin rotation of its head and neck.

In Which You Are Disappearing from the Natural World Obviously

Lather on the winter coat of the gray horse:
a dapple. From your fingers, the pink apple

of your palm, heart-of-palm with its life-river,
its fate-river, its blood-river. I mean it's a strange thing—

shadow of your hair on the wall, winter wheat
and then the tall, flat plain of your back and thigh.

But then, the fields are always fairest in a flood-plain,
swimming in the cream, that broth which is the fog

poured into the valley by the sun. Wake up too warm,
march the floorboards, throw out the screens.

Put your mind into the air. City street, aisle of brick.
The cat more robot than animal, the breeze

like an exertion, like *product.* Dew shines on the hoods
of the cars, braided up and down the street.

Paraded larches, geisha-gowned, and then corrals
of *lawn,* ceramic planters, eternal hostas.

Heart like a mop, soaking up the water of the real world,
of the real world. Lost,

lost, but then,
you have become so awesome at faking it.

Institution Pool

Here at the shallow end of yourself,
you find you have been *streamlined*.

You cannot find the tickle-bone in the fury.
You cannot find the face of your child in the face of your child,

in the face of the beauty, speaking, her hand
on the arm of a man. What do you think of our programs? he asks.

As if the helping was good.
As if the aged and infirm could gather into something profound,

with proper feed and water, blossom into nodding, permanent
     assent.
Sweat slips its slick, heavy tongue

down your back, between the bone and fat.
The pool is an empty, icy pendant,

on the green bosom of the estate.
You cannot find disappointment in the weariness.

So this is what she will become.
And there, there, that is what you will be,

a crooked lady in a blue dress, tilted
on a bench, her wispy hair askew, eyes blearily

congested, corridors blanked out by fog.
As if the helping was wrong. As if we were meant

to go out, bent over the same turnip row
we, previously, sowed, and then hoed,

and then, at the very end, pickled and stored.
So someone could have them who needs them more.

And There, That Was the Middle

Listening to you hum *Mellow My Man* by the Roots &
I am imagining the moths of late July stroking the screen

as if it were a sheet of Braille. They are called cabbage white
butterflies & all damage aside, I love the way they float

at dusk, eager to mate. So I know about how you feel,
wasting your life. The closet-secret of your bright potential,

those first chess games, organic chemistry. I imagine
in those days you were happy—after all our bodies were young,

we made love in dormitory beds. It makes sense to me that just now
    you have learned to be fearless and to express

how angry you are. You have pressed yourself against a wall
for a decade and still it will not move. How heart-rending

that just now I recall the Hyde Park laundromat that first
hot day of June. 90 degrees, the suds, the scent of folded blue jeans.

O your promise to me has been fulfilled so many times,
I cannot distinguish each from each.

The dusk, it fills with wings.
The ghostly paper, so eager for a word.

O It Rises

It takes a thickness to be human,
a pond & pine-water sort of thickness,

set-up like jelly. It does not take as much gall
as you think it will & only one kidney

& no tactics at all, not really.
Most of the time we are too slight for it anyway—

we are gray little thrushes
instead of iron ingots & we sway & we sway.

Just like that, cussing in the street
at the neighbor with the brilliant security light.

Can't even leave the curtains open.
& your husband says he's not a feminist any longer, he's not,

which you should have seen appearing,
a gray thread in the braid, in the twine.

& now it makes sense, a sad flexibility, feet in stirrups.
See most of the time we are grass-shrimp, full of chitin

& we are red balloons & love is a ceiling against which
most of the time we are slight as those balloons,

slight as a memorandum about coffee supplies or
open-toe sandals. & suddenly you know the heaviness

of words lost in the enormous bottom of a bell.
Well you are lifting it, you are lifting it.

Everything Sends

For Andrew Joron

The toaster speaks to the sun
to planets

to a telephone
& this is faith   in the value of chatter

Above us, driven by invisible chords & sequences
the air fills with

the brine of homeland security, sapphire sendings
of clock radios

Even naked we are not naked enough
The room empties from us

unfurls   atmosphere uncomely, tethered
to an interface

We don't need words for happiness
We don't need words for wayment

This quivering signal like tossed pebbles,
unstopped by mixing fog, sleet, hail,

unstopped by the implicit edge of night
The goodness of our hearts   unruly skeins of webby silence

which we tutor with fingers
buttons tools

Referential

I am happy to know that the lord is law and love and love is that weird ten minutes late at night when you have to decide whether you're going to fuck or just act like you're mad that you aren't going to fuck when secretly you're happy to have your body to yourself for ten minutes, your own stillness, there, in that slender rectangle where you practice the poses of eternity, supine, and I am happy that we are past the point of looking into one another's faces all the time, so that when we do pass too closely, when we stop in the space between the bathroom door and the basement door, suddenly our breath is basic religion, there's unstoppable pressure in our ears, as if we were careening up the Adirondacks, hillside by hillside and look, I am happy that in bed you sometimes call me a whore because it takes the sting out of how ridiculous you think I am with money and I'm happy that the overpass hums our way, the trains murmur just below the cliffside because there is never uncomfortable silence and satellites are bright enough to be our moons when we don't feel the need to explain to one another, to footnote mistakes, and all that, all that I am with you I am in spite of you, errant creative power, each choice veering from one you made before, already always, and I am happy, anyway, as luck would have it, fucking stupid and happy to know that this is not the kind of city you mess with, this is not the kind of team you discount early in the season and even if *together* is half dirty command, half article, I am happy to know it's both of us injuring, breaking, and then, so sweetly, in the dark, fumbling at nothing, at nothing.

It May Taste Sweet

By this I mean the moon, whipped milk
spilled crescent

on the cold kitchen tile.
We thought that this stone-fired

brick and bourbon city
would be the perfect place for us to grow

slowly less starry-eyed.
And that groaning America would be the perfect place

for us to acquire a pair of matching Jettas.
Over time I would lose the threshing song of combines,

the rape-music of heavy cars, the yeasty Budweiser breath
of men who, I mean, were made so much better

by churchyards and tenderloin. And if not that, at least a warm
    kitchen
would help us survive, the Steelers and Call of Duty,

beerball on the new dining room table.
But it turns out the moon just returns and returns.

It seems we stand so far apart, I might as well be
a threshing room floor and you the great city boom,

an industrial sweetheart, a factory shirtwaist.
I might as well be the on the other side

of that moon, and you, standing there, saying *just*
come on over here, why can't you come over here?

Grandmother

She was a good woman who worked hard. *All that work,*
the toothy uncles sigh. The hard work wore her.

Like a flat, smocked housedress, like a brown heeled shoe.
And then, the breakdown. Like a produce truck, she stuttered, guttered,

and spilled. The neighborhood, all cabbages and smoke.
Her head a froth of thinnish, snow-white thread.

Does that clock tick in *my* head? *O no,* they've said,
she just was very, very poor. And a saint, as they now recall it,

with hindsight and sober observation. She sewed the little pants
they wore and made them go to church. *Maybe it was her heart*

that broke? They won't joke about the firing squad
inside her head, marching with suspenders and hats,

aiming direct into the center of the brain. Those kinds of things might bear
their fruit into the blood, sweet grapes of gloom, clustered thickly

in the back of the throat, hunkered in the head,
souring to a bitter, moldy wine. A net of bad proteins encircling

each subsequent generation. O drink of me, the wrist sings. Let sunlight
catch me afire, the blood hums. Let me run through the orchard,

into the knocked-out fields, along the irrigation ditches,
to the oak wood where the foxes hide,

the fishers and the martens. *Grandmother,* I might say, throwing back
the shutters of the little house,

you look strange to me, but so familiar, and then sit waiting
for the shrouded beast to leap and take me.

19

Beach House

The surfaces of the rooms are veiled, quilted, waxed
and the wind in every season, at every hour

sighs on the staircase, slips beneath the hemmed ridge.
All this pluming, extravagance

confers comfort, makes new the very notion of *staying*.
Are we here? Yet?

Sure, the language of that breeze,
a vein of flippancy, guides us through lamplit corridors,

brings us forward, ever forward
and somewhere in the yard,

a hand pump divulges the slippery scorn of the earth,
its bilious heartbeat

and the lawn floods with a sweet, dense fog
the color of banana cream

We who linger in the tissue, the barathea,
the wet linen with its safflower sheen

find such wafting, floating oneirology
that we forget the clothespins, the line, the work of laundry,

and instead shiver, interpolated by fingertips,
held between bodies, our night the fullness of a cavern,

the released seedling calling out this one impossible
riddle   call me who is the calling

Spring Cleaning

Women put their white cloths to the glass of a thousand windows.
Let's call that sunrise.

Do you know how many wolves are out there in the dawn?
Do you know the motion it takes to bring them into sight?

We have let all that slip through us, a spectral poignancy.
Now nothing, nothing, nothing, nothing. O honey,
honey, I am not some good live thing. It is still

night out there. I have just tried to explain the great joy
of creeping around the country house from the outside,
sidling unseen from window to window, the joy of being

absent. I have been trying to calculate that joy
all of my life. I am reminded of that every time
I see a piece of newspaper crumpled.

Remember the white volcano of kissing the wrong woman?
Every single day of your life?

This morning, with strange clarity, I am sure it is still the night.
I am certain that the work these women do is hard and pointless.
With long gestures and pressure, with exact motion, worried,
they bring their hands up again and again. Let's call that living.

From the Reformed Presbyterian Theological Seminary on the First Warm Day in March, a Man Comes Running in a White T-Shirt

I know the home of my thoughts because,
just then, it settles. *Zing.* Like the well-dowser's
hazel wand ticks, ticks,
and at last, dips.

At the bus-stop, black women in yellow scarves,
young boys with their tallit fringe. We are all

so obviously thinking only of worldly things. Sense appeals to every
organism—one warm pass, two dandelions bloom

in frost-charmed grass. One quick shadow overhead,
the sparrows shut their mouths.

So we are always waiting when the deeper need enters,
when the aftershock suggests to us

that we are not entirely alive. When the baby bites
through the electrical cord. When the bird
slams into the window.

When the hand claws at the throat, at the place where the heart
has just threatened to break. I think of *you,*
this being all the heaven I will know.
This being how you always move.

O man, delicate man, with dark thoughts, bursting forth,
at last reformed.

Teaching Me to Shoot

Barefoot on the raw green silk of the lawn.
Beyond us, in the fat, far distance

the corn tasseled and swung, needing no shove.
And beyond that, the edging of old trees, copse

upon copse, oaks and maples, pinched and swelled
like an elastic waistband.

You visited upon me the grave, dark body of the rifle
A serious infant, capable of so much shouting.

O father, sunsick and squinting, I raised it to my shoulder.
I touched its little click, its metallic organ

And then how it buckled and arched, how it made
its own will known.

On the fencepost, the cardboard shearing, penetrated.
And out, resounding out, the tucked boom,

a contracting throat-muscle, torn from my own body,
naming me a danger to cats and rats

and men across the fields,
where Echo's body lay, still singing.

Returned

The white iron-notched curio cabinet is empty of purpose,
in your dead father's house. Someone has filled it with dozens
of stained white coffee mugs.

The first intervention is one called heartbeater.
The second intervention is one called deepswimmer.

Once the lake was a pretty good dreamer.
Now a glossy spill of gasoline resurfaces the complex,
woven green.

Once your mother found you old-fashioned suitcases
at a garage sale, heavy & awkward, with wooden stomachs.

Now your stepmother pours one cup of coffee after another,
over nothing, into nothing.

The consequence of all that surfless, swimming nothing
is a spouse, a house, a kitchen mouse.

This is also the prize for avarice.

Nobody catches us at anything beautiful.

You stare at the girl riding the bus-pole, her left thigh
    hitched up tight, her leg crooked to leave her hands free,
pulling back her ponytail.

The third intervention is one called nonstoplaughter.

Entropy isn't what it used to be.

There's something too similar about *slaughter* and *laughter*.

April Snow

—after Lorine Niedecker

Within the tin, darkdrop bucket
milk sings *where is the white sky?*

Tracking quietly like a clapboard fence,
sanctified snow,

saxony snow.
Thought is snow.

Winter has thrown
this curve of sweet alyssum,

peppery white.
Yes, last night's rain

milky in the bucket.
Remember how the water

filled and gouged?
Each rock a spout

from the crumbling steps
of your front porch,

an alluvial fan
from where the world

runs out of sky
—the paper trade

is slow today
& everyday.

Turkish March

At dawn you would march your fingers,
cracked and stout, shake your wrists
and hammer down. The Turks, you knew,
were headed out into the corn.
Those janissary birds, so devout,
following the sounds in and out.

Woke we, being five. Curved, we. First
upon us, the hammered sense.
The undulate moan. A carving bird.
A dove of horn. Bringing water home,
bringing the flood to the basin.

With hurry, you would shake us.
Foot on the pedal, you would chase us
from the harvesting of a dream.
In a gold way of breath,
you would bring your march
of death, the arrangement
of a holy lord who, worshipped thus,

might fly past us in the war,
might let us fall in love after all.
By then we could see. The dust
rafting down the waterfall of sunlight.
Blue stains on the corner of the sheet.

Is there an absolute justice
we cannot see? Is there a good thing,
caught in the nest of the ear, tweeting
dearly, blessed and blessed?
O on the near approach we'd float,
waiting for your crashing-down.

Amsterdam

those fingers   blue and dark
the charcoal harkening   to paper of my breast
and went around it

and became an animal
avocative lizard   primordially winged
tongues   as pterodactyls

is this beautiful? no
and no flowering   but a brutal
sugar, as from fallen, bruised fruit

and is that the secret of my life, now?
married, made a woman?
that laziness, that wreaking

as milk from teat, as bile from duct
the morning throat, blue Amsterdam
I am not, you know

beyond, in this memory
superhuman hearing
tram wheels
someone puking in the street

after after
this is what it means to be divided
& foundering is such good hurt

o my country   I can see your walls
streets, green fields, character
marriage, baby, middle management

an almond tree in early bloom
the tight, near-white bud
bit by frost, closing-down

something *made* continues
but also vanishes
like the wet streets into so much fog

deeply, deeply advent, a Whitsunday
with forgiveness as baptismal gown

II

Pain Questionnaire[2]

Tell me, Philoctetes, on a scale of 1 to 10,
can you describe the pain again?

Circle the words that describe it best.
Does it feather out, like a wren in nest?

Does it flicker, quiver, pulse, throb, beat?
Pound, jump, flash, shoot, heat?

Does it prick or bore, drill or stab?
Does it lacinate, cut, pinch, or grab?

Compare it to the worst headache you've ever had.
O dear cave, you call. I have gone mad

with it, with the hollow world and shelf of stone.
No. Stay here with me. Tell me its hue and tone.

Does it decrease when you lie down?
Pool around your feet like a volcanic bridal gown?

If I am a stranger, what is this pain to you?
A friend? Relation? A home you deeply knew?

You call farewell to the wet meadow.
How describe it at dusk? At dawn? In the snow?

How does that compare to the pain you feel
when the hurt is at its lightest, when you kneel

in the fog, in the dawn, against the back wall
half-dead from cold, waiting for the birds to call?

O Philoctetes, to numb it, what is best?
Intercourse, massage, sleep or rest?

Pain Has No Future but Itself

Rain at night builds a cave
in the house.

Who do you say you were?
I must have felt you pass

me by. Not tonight honey.
The bats are lavender and white,

kicking against the side
of the brain, a shrill hurrying

I can't explain. I was walking into the woods,
wearing red.

The rain lay down at my feet,
it purred and kitted,

swung its weepy tail.
You've been here before, I can see.

The humor seems familiar to you,
the dank air, the thread

of chill in the corridor.
Where was I? O, the red scarf,

the rainboots, the sour stars.
And pain on the left side. Pain on the right.

Something spoke to me, which had always,
always, known my name.

Now I can't say if it hurt to see things
laid out that way, boned

like a fish, the pale tissue
articulated

into fathomless form.
If I knew it was growing in me,

at the same time . . .wait,
I would take it with me if I could.

But there is such a cost, a closet
or cupboard of cost.

Are you here again? Already?
Or has it been forever?

The wolf's teeth are seeds
planted in my brain.

All night, the gnawing, the bones.
In the cave, they glow white,

bloom like anemone, with their strange
fungal fruit.

Cuticle

Pain proves the body,
Pricks and burrs.

It is an organ
Of your other organs,
A small cramped heart
In your hand,

Which has done too much,
Which has done so much work.

The kidney of your ear,
Which aches and yellows.
The lung in your lung,
Which punches and flattens,
Punches hard.

You looked for this, didn't you,
At times? In the least, you felt
Something which hurts
Is a natural cantilever of the soul,
Balancing it just inside
The confines of bone and tissue,
Suspended in the boiling body.

From One Thing, Another

"I had neither hate nor pity. The situation was urgent...."

— Paul Aussaresses, French torturer[2]

The chair is an agent of pain, though
    it does not have agency. It is unyielding.
As is the garden hose. A toilet. A red lamp.
Towel bar. Bedsheet. Metal spoon.

Look, we can build a little house of this torture,
we can fill its cabinets with knives and forks.
With buckets and bathtubs. And you will be alone
in this house, alone with your thoughts,
with the hours, or beetles, black and scurrying.
No, you will never be alone in this house.

Decades after the skin has knitted, knotted,
burled its way over and into each hurt,
you will have become another woman
with a shopping bag, squeezing carrots.
And he will be, somewhere distant,
a grandfather who likes to fish in the summer.

At the change of light which comes
near the end of the day, both of you will stop
of a sudden, will half-turn, and see in the quiet
arrangement of chair-legs and tables, of cords
and curtain rods, of lamp-bulbs and the chains
that ignite them, a sinister echo, a flashing

dark animal. One that skulks through this house
of shouting that straddles two worlds, two eras,
in which you both pace your separate-but-united chambers,
dream your dreams, fold your errant laundry,
perform your nightly ablutions.

2. Brass, Martin. "Torture to Prevent Terrorism?" Military.com. N.p., 2001.
Web. 13 June 2016.

The Scalded Map

"Sickness shows us the border that is skin" – Alberto Rios

Let us say there is a map, somewhere, of all that binds
and constricts the vessels, all that pinches the nerves

and suspends us in the great storm of it, waving
our paper arms like cut-out dolls. Let us say

some of it is old country, land much-worked, now spoiled.
And some is new pain, the borders just sketched in.

Let us say you have walked there, on the red dividing line
between the country of my hurts and yours.

And between us is a common lake, this blue hurtling,
this ever-shifting body, an interred blankness

that some interpret as darkness. We have sown it
with wildflowers all around, with oleander and rosary peas,

with foxglove and monkshood and yew.
And I have said you cannot cross it, you cannot come

to my side, nor I to yours. But we will meet in the middle,
in the night. Rocking, intertwined. And ride its secret tides

until we feel the rhythm. And take it with us back to our own
unfathomable places, our caves and brilliant cities.

Job

"The womb forgets them, the worm feasts on them; evil men are no longer remembered but are broken like a tree." (Job 24:20)

I lived in that age and for a thousand years was dead.
And for another thousand alive again.
Social pain, they call it now.

Then, there was no landscape for this, no myleogram, no stain or
  electric pulse.

But now. Pull the bone back from the muscle, the muscle back
  from the bone, prick the boil, swell the neck, stitch the uneven
  hem of the foot. It fires a new light in the brain. They can map
  this pain. Alright, they can map it. They can then make it better.

And so, you, the living, do not fear me. I have never had shade.
I have never believed in the blazing wood,
the broth of fire poured into the breath.

Dragon, you will say, a thousand years from now.
Dragons lived. Here is evidence.
The scan shows imaginal discs in the pain-brain.
Gauze-feathered wings in the heartbreak,
horns and claws in the splintering ache.

Social pain, the doctor says, *is not
really pain at all. But something else.
We need a new word for all that, Job,*

Tell me, my soul, like leaves in a wood,
a million folded pressure points, brightening in sunlight?
Pain does point the way.
Any question, any answer and all the leaves say *yes*.

Translation

There is no way to translate Philoctetes'[3] agony. *Oh!*
someone has suggested. Another has written *Ah! Ah! Ah!*

But Philoctetes speaks in tongues. In phonemes
ripped from the throat of the earth, from the muddy

ciliates, the sacred sparks of silica, the mossy slime.
Father, you, too, spoke in tongues and so I know

that elongated speech and what it means. As you knelt
by Danny, the dead boy in the road: ashikalama amay amay.

As blood fountained from the cut, shot forth through
all the life force that was in you: baray shadokanipannan.

As you buried the half-made child, her head no bigger
than the round of a teaspoon, akama alaiaka ala akama akai.

So when Philoctetes moans and writhes, when something
comes to his mouth, more like froth or foam than a word,

I know it is the spirit of the hurt that lifts and wedges its weight
between teeth and gum, chortles and hums in the cheek,

secretes itself with something similar to ecstasy, but not,
I promise, the same as ecstasy. Not, I promise, the same

as anything felt before. There is no word for something that only
you feel, in you. That cannot be transferred or transgressed,

which does not require another's participation. Which is only
a clove sucked into the soul, a numbing which stabs and burns,

3. "Pain Questionnaire" and "Translation" reference the story of Philoctetes,
who survived in exile on Lemnos, alone, with a festering wound, for ten
years, as recorded in Homer's *Iliad.*

and cannot be waylaid. Father, it never comes to me as it did
to you. The spirit does not press onto my heart or head, does not

demand that I beg for the dead. Does not try to pray the skin
knit together, the heart to beat. I cannot say I know it at all,

though I've heard it so many times before.
Apappapai, papa papa papa papai.

Snare

Count the time as you normally would, but watch
for the arc. Smooth as breath, the undulate rhythm

awakes. Gut snares stretch. The brushes for it
have learned to live with your panic.

The felt-tipped wings of the apple moth
respond to your tickling gasp. They respond to your

feeling. The prick-point, the tch tch tch of pique.
a percussive counting from inside. Life will make

a mathematician of you yet. Somewhere, Mr. Hassan,
your geometry teacher, with his boxer's paws, is shaking

with laughter. Because pain's the only shape
that fits your heart, now, the only shape of the drum

you hear. The passage, for one like you, was always
going to be dear. So clutch your little coin tight.

Let the moth flap her wings. Let the blood hammer home.
Somewhere distant, o,

that other beating, too. As if two shapes
vibrating at the same frequency.

Fever

red is infection, first bloom
of deeper malady and there are

fields interlaced, watermelon snow
the brassy tufts of fox fur caught

on barbed wire   look, fire
has been here and your cheeks perk

heat like a tea-kettle   you are getting
close to a boil, look the skin

erupts, the winter brings out roses
on your sweet, too-thin upper lip

the fox is there again, down in the ditch
waiting for a chance

and this is the theater of red, the velvet rope
of the human body on deep blue sheets

the wild strawberry, too small to cut
or bite or share, it must be taken whole

it must be fought by the body along the way
but also embraced   deconstructed

the way a sonata can be unhinged, bass
from melody, hand from hand

the fox with her deep black hole is waiting
in the snow and your body implies heat

wherever it goes   we stand there
too long in the shower steam

until everything we meant evaporates
what did we have on our skin?

has our hot blood cooled? have we cooled?
and why is the sound coming now, the growl

which both beseeches and protests
just lie on your back with your arms here

and there and with the red flag in your chest
across your rising, raving dream

a soft, faint thing thuds and skids
the snow fails at impression

and there's nothing but ozone, then
and cornfields and everything imagined

White Powder

On Tuesday a light dusting.
Wednesday, wind and fog

      disseminate.

And then it's hard to breathe;
a second, a third thumb

appearing and   *have we changed?*

That thin layer of dust on the window pane
is transformative;   the old house
has become a block of ice, requires
skates to approach. The thin blades
of those skates become
like feet   right before . . .   *Wait.*

Now we can fly.

No, we were not paranoid.

Two women in Starbucks stir and spoon.
     And I said no we don't need two microwaves.

But the damage is already done;
a horn juts from the bone of the forehead
which is the frontal bone, the boss
and lord. The wet flecks on my windshield
invoke such sorry memory—   game preserve

in late autumn, the scent of burnt coffee,
the way, when touching
the carapace of the upright piano
dust motes rose and spun,
the way live yeast
in a warm kitchen can arise and become feral.

Is there an almighty   in the fine fabric
of poison that the crop-dusters lay down?
or the envelope
that you opened?
Or the pollen from the paper birch?

Is there a promise
in the febrile sleep   the heat that is taken away
            by the other body,
that heals   the first body?

Poinsettia

i.

Red bracts, like this month's blood. Like the lost one, slipping down my inner thigh while we sat watching that Nirvana documentary. Emptiness? Yes. Yet, I see in that center star a kind of navigable promise. Where the cat has chewed the coal-bright red a pool of black now spreads. She is sick, heaves, her numb tongue thick in her little mouth. Which has done the most damage to the other? My husband opens the door late at night. The rain, the squeak of his wet shoes on the stair. Probably it's just as well. Probably that glossy wood, dry from years of radiant heat, sealed by wax, is crying out, stirred by the small, thin droplets. To grow, to be something better, isn't that the only thing? The poinsettia requires an exact amount of sunlight to deepen, to fire off each delicate rocket, to become more than just another a roadside weed. I know how that feels, the waiting, I mean, that precise voodoo.

ii.

Like blood on ferns, the poinsettias on the landing of the stair. White cat curled, a fawn in the center of that poignant raft. Some people say the world will end because of the sun, or because men can buy guns. The *long count* is what we call our prediction of the future. To make the poinsettia full and bright, it is infected with a kind of blight, a phytoplasmic shot. Not so differently the clot of blood which surrounds its seed. An energy abounds in fevered times, a little hurt to make anything grow. Mere chance which makes some bloom from sickness, some decay.

iii.

To cry on cue. Watch White Christmas. Change your Facebook status to *hurting, but in the holiday spirit*. As if that's not enough, the Steelers execute one sloppy play after another. Is it harder to throw a pass or raise a child? Is it possible to win by wanting? After all. After all. Now we have to think, all the time, about what it means to be human. About what it means to eat truly organic arugula. Now we have to think about if this is the right moment for gun control. It seems, this year, the poinsettias are larger than ever before. Waist-high, they wait for you outside the elevator with something preda-tory in their festive flashlight. No more raised than a weed—next year, who knows, they'll be the size of compact cars. And while ev-erything gets larger & sunnier & sunnier & larger, while the North Pole turns into a swimming pool, old pains persist. Knees ache, hearts. So much, so much, that it feels right to keep a plant which is made to die, made to dry, to glory still, despite the birth and death, despite the economic boom which has just followed the downturn. *Why are you still up?* You ask your husband on the stairs. He's stand-ing there, the moonlight glib and drunk, and next year maybe this will be brighter & brighter, too.

III

Flora – Winter

i.

The heart is a thrashing machine, a wrecker, a snowplow
on the county line and hour after hour
it makes its sad clearing, it tries to push away
blue stains on the ice, the age of your face,
the wet facets of honeycomb fastened to the barbed wire

ii.

In Indiana, the creeks run
through ice-plates, shifting to take up new courses.

In Pittsburgh, the nickel-colored avenues
advance under white veils
like good country girls
wearing all their wedding linen at once.

iii.

Taking the turnpike back to the city, long breaths in the sunrise.
Suet for brown-headed cowbirds, the nuthatches and creepers.

My mother calls from a land-line, crackled & soft
as old leather gloves. *Digging out for hours*, she says,
you just, just missed it.

iv.

Under the Highland Park Bridge, the Allegheny is white-lashed.
The blue-gray caulk on boats,
doves beneath the fir trees, rustling,

wrestling. If memory serves me,
the early wanting is always the strongest,
the early milk, pulled from the teat
the early bus, grinding its gears.

We begin in the money.
The foreman explains when it's permissible
to second-guess the robot.

We begin in the grease,
the hands of a neighbor returning from the mouth of the truck,
Mara licks butter from the knife.

v.

Outside the clinic, the forgettable imprint
of wild turkey & deer

in the snow.
Now men go, and women go

and eventually
the wind lifts the snow.

vi.

It's become pointless to stack the cordwood
against the wind-break fenceline.

Gas is cheap.
The bricks in the chimney are tumbling from the inside,
banking up the path to the sky.
Nothing breathes in there.

Mara wants a beauty school in a box,
she wants Dreams to Dresses II.

Whatever birds are left, numb shadowy things,
kettle and wheel, anxious, practicing

for the bilious waves of tropical storms, for night skies
where they'll ride above the enterprise of the world.

Together, Mara says.
I want to look at this to-geth-er

vii.

In the winter garden, liver greens, collard, dandelion yellow,
frost-blackened kale.

Spore teeth, split green tonsils.
Take the freeze and define

wet taphonomy, thunderhead, bolus
in the iced bed of civilization,
the cultivated hedgebank,
sponge borings and waxed paper.

A word stirs the world, they say, but the wind, just now
kicked up only this fine mold,
as frost, as anoxia.

Protecting your pearls, arranging the soft moth
of your scarf wings
a fabric, a feather
between anther and ether
a plant cuticle caught in starbeam

and human only in format,
we go along then, go along then
anywhere
caught on one another, carried by one another.

Flora — Spring

i.

last year's menace, these brown runners, seed pods, trumpet vine
a breme compendium   riotous, now, in all the beds
and valleys, the lethargy of August which,

in April, must be railed against   each length
of turned soil worked by hand   a woman

with blonde shoots herself, kneeling   dishing up
soil near the charred sweetbay.

ii.

loose petals   a pink tabernacle   the kind of murmured paradise
you said you could live without,
if not without clean laundry, changed lightbulbs

how can a person spend a whole life without thinking of god
or macaroni and cheese

without exhausting perfectly inexhaustible angles
casting for that backwards glance

if the heart is a threshing machine and the soul a planter
what comes between them but
those time-weary sunflowers, plump with prime verbs?

iii.

kidney-shaped   in the sour earth
dark organs return   and return   and return

to perpetuate the body
its uric wash,   germinal
and finite

but oh the bottom rung of the ladder to heaven is still heaven

iv.

what has to be taken from the ground?
what has to be surrendered?

the breath, the heaved sigh   occasionally we pretend
to be here with one another

we pretend   here

while it takes forever to keep wondering   no
finally

but here?

v.

the seed   patron saint of bad ideas   bad marriages
an ode to estrangement   on the porch, a clay pot

the pieces that still, somehow   understand what it means
to hold   they spoon up rainfall

for ourselves, the sections   middle, softness
upper hardness   at the many bud-points, at the branches

we're all deployment

vi.

last week your mother arrived with a box of your things
she is making her way   resurfacing your agenda

with black tar, with old worries, paper,
prom champagne flutes,
          trophies

you are resurfacing the strawberry bed, clearing away the old straw,
snipping runners   a dozen thumb-sized blossoms

like seed pearls above the black earth

what kind of tormentor has bound them, enrobed them,

thrust them out?

as irritant, time has its pros and cons
                        I have hardly remembered you,
o young heart,   and now I can just as easily
set you aside

vii.

what remains?

I mean   it's out now, its tender red leaves
forming an umbrella, lifting the entire enterprise of the world

I mean   can't it be that praying
is something you can keep doing
even after you know there's nothing to pray for?

viii.

branch to a thousand branches
speaks coral,

wolf's milk
fungus

coltsfoot by the pond
branch to a thousand branches

lift
up thy head

Flora — Summer

i.

Oleander, wasn't this? A place to sink?

First hatched shadow, a squiggle
raporous

an owl, then a pale
moth

then
            will it catch us?

By our own diction, we are measurable,
we are running the numbers,
pitching low, fast.

ii.

The stars move out in eclipse formation.
On the black plane of the trampoline,

heat still slowly lifting
lifting

interposes
limb and limb

a formulation of mass, a heaviness
which, singly, we would not claim

iii.

fat rose
a burst whisper and then   just there

where the mouth
hisses

hard shower of clean water
the slick faucet

and brick beneath
bare feet

iv.

psalmody over-lying salt-water peat
inlet, bay

an hour from Cape May Point
Matthew rolls the window open
and our lungs contract

then the open
morning, which is water
spatterdock and cordgrass

our bodies, for all their work and usefulness,
now soft with purpose
like so much washed flannel

flat water
small docks floating in sea lavender

v.

white flat of our thighs
these re-entered bays
and re-entered and re-entered

bed's flat pillows at midnight
lying-in like jetties

human as that anonymous ship
now entirely engulfed by darkness,

the sound of a distant horn section
a scrap of net fluttering

vi.

each color one brush
reed canary grass and sunset's late breaking tide

the body empties when the body empties
there's very little, at this stage, which can be done

milk glass like fish scales and fish scales like milk glass
voices cross-follow voices up the walnut banister

fragile as speckled eggs
aim low or you won't get anywhere at all

nevertheless, fecundity is omnipresent
the fish explode at night, thousands and thousand
every ghost crab, every root, every verb perishes,
blossoms like there's no difference between

Flora — Autumn

i.

Who listens? The janissary birds, so devout?
A carving bird? A dove of horn?

Marked plots disintegrate, the street a racket
of mow/mow/snow/snow.
Here, there belt-line, rust-belt, turnpike.

The alien river, pushing up, pulling its sweater of red leaves.

O the silvery   tucked body   strange body
of the river   I am learning
I have learned it is

I have found it is like a woman, the contrary curve,
its tenderness to the geese, embracing them
by the legs and hearts
and then, arbitrarily,
its violence to the drunk boater

ii.

The refugees, stranded on the sea, cling to the deep-water well.
At some point, it has become just money.

It has become the wild red zinnia, returned
from the first frost, still glowing.

It is just money.   The bricks elide and slide.
The house is growing downstream.
The cars need new belts and timing,

well, timing is precious.

iii.

Oil in the water, money in the water. Don't forget about
the bucket, ill-drained, which has, all summer collected
   mosquitoes
& black fish   & frog-bit   & hornwort, anacharis.

Grace, by its good name, all hems and stems. The snails dig down.
The fish belly.

From the neck of the word, o health
it is poured. Years & years
of that crippling insurance.
Disability, life, bowl of milk, bowl of cream.
O the cat, helped, finds the hearth a dungeon.
The oil, slick, finds itself carrying scales, bones, and feathers.

iv.

Grimoire of red leaves, next door the beagle
lunges at foes,   her throat a bass drum.

Nothing divided, nothing distant.   The world crowds
and chains like rust on the rail.

It is not like your book. It is not the story.

A man sends half of his money to some
crumbled concrete in the desert.
Be something, he says. I can make you home again.

In the city there is something
fruitless about searching.   At midnight,

deer walk in the street, eat the rotting crabapples
from half an inch of fresh-fallen glow,
their ears in the prithee position.

Teleology of the Atl-Atl

Skywhip
    sought imprint

driving as it did
    bi-face opalescent, self-murmur
    -ing into the shoulder   through the cage

of words, a breakneck bird-dart
    which nothing really,   not really   nothing

really understood until that   half-caught *zing*

a passthrough realm
    of organs, fish-scales, knuckles

this buttend charmstone
    worked bone   worked & iterated   & worked

arriving like weather, like bloodscent
    a residual thing, lashed   to air's scrollwork

rolling in rolling in crimson   takes the breath
    out of
        anything containing breath

shell-hook, an antler
                            of all glistening particles

powered, en-quickened
                        vibrating wedge intersecting

    pinwheels

Teleology of Dark Fibre

\

wood thrush digging for beetles
in the garden urn
sings his bup-bup-bup
into the caliginous silence
saltboxes, brick boxes, dripping eaves
like so much Bucchero earthenware
in the duskafter, just after.

\

what is wrapped now
around the husk of a sound, dispatched
cabled to air cocooned in the sheer length of nothing
bearing me, as you did
into that dim estuary
into a semiotics of grass and gravel
blown ocean foam   runner beans

\

braiding sheaths   of walnut-floss, girl-hair
teaching the faith muscle
the sweet muscle
as if hair does not convolute
harden   from silk to twine
fray and frizz
blanch

\

wondered, still, a word?
where can it really go?

\

a cave in the center of the lilac bush
that glazed cambium
which, grafted, clings, combines

so the lavender paintbrushes
draped, enrobed in Goethe's purple
flushed cheeks, dissolving knots of wind and shadow
indeed, all memory will end
but, witchknotted,   will also endure
in the haymow,
as seedy guesswork, engrailed in viscera,
vomit, decay, thin
intensely moving   strands of apophatic haste
it is not what was
it is not whatever it will be
how to avoid speaking
how to   avoid whatever you've asked for
if someone is shouting for you   if hate is calling your name
it is also love   for it returns you from nothing

\

time can be cut and rejoined
he said   the chessman purposed towards me,
brandishing a new humiliation
meaning these dense systems of prayer, rummage sales,
the noise of combines running late at night in August, striving
     against bad weather

all that, he said, is warm
but you are ice water
can I not save
one from the pitiless wave
it is not something saved
it is not something separate
lost botany of this moment   supine, fingers
over the coils of spoon mooss
this feigned succumbing   half-tuned

\

dusk above Ponte Valentre
day below
two vinerows rule,   moored like ships

to an encroaching dim

\

what? wrapped now, a straight bundle, you housefly
and just above, in the bunk, the jiggle
of someone jerking of

\

a vestige, barely linguistic
of warm water
first steam
cell-pods   popping, singing
in any presence, such a concrete comfort

\

o now we're far back enough that we might begin again,
say voices from the dining room
a whispery thirst with the same pigment as paralysis
even an impression has weight and it,
now, hangs from the branches
of the peach tree
hums with an empty message

Teleology of Febreze

The room smells of sex and buffalo sauce
& there are a dozen ouchless ponytail holders
in the crevasse between bed and wall
& suddenly the image of the house is so important
& indicates success you don't feel because
of damp ceilings, mildew in the closet
& the way the house fills with the scent of fabric softener

& when the two of you tangle,
as if in a linnet's nest
at least you don't think of yourself
as a snake until the next day
you don't think of her lizard tongue,
her dark-summer irises until she's gone

I should like my house to be similar to that of the ocean wind.

& that sentence may have a heartbeat, but it is
the dresser drawer that has a scent
Your great-grandfather built it
& it smells of furniture wax & cedar forest
& suddenly the silk is gone, her skirts are made
of pillow ticking, of drapes & the room is always
in the almond, always shoe-polish and azalea

Are you certain you really *need* this?

Her hair, where it was bound up wet,
smells of feathers and basements
& her body's warm milk-smell,
the baby cooling its bare bottom
on the sheet beside her while you stay there, too,
drowsily letting the Sunday sun teach you
a good lesson about purpose

This is the ocean, you thought, kissing the salt
from her fingers & just like that, the house is back
to its murderous ways, bloodscent
in the anteroom, mice working their flat-feet
between the floorboards, down the chimney
& something in her backwards look
suggests that she has begun to put things *second*
to reserve the *first*

A is for apple, your daughter reads,
her feet gray from running in the garden
even though you have long forsaken
gods of your fathers, gardens of your fathers

& suddenly your wife has done something unusual
sliced through the pears and her thumb,

that *almost-nothing,* that *not-quite*
juice spilling on her fingers
later in bed, you will not taste her
for fear, for fear

Teleology of the Clock

On certain days, lithe creatures stalked the green,
boys pitched pennies into caps.

They called it the fair.

Once was a cricket, in a ribbon cage.
Once was a therapy couch, all leather sockets,
all worn honeycombs. Once was a gray
Ford Fairmont, rain on the turnpike,
garden intervals, straight as rulers.

Draw a line, says the cricket. On the other side,
will I be free?

A new word is made to hold the leaves, boil the water.
When will you meet me?

A wedding dress answers. The windier it grows,
you know, a change in its snail-shell.
All day in the gorges the sun fell

where it worked, tossed its gold
on the oat kernels, brambles, and rosebay.
It also worked a star moving sideways,
a crevice where words fell.

A mháithrín, a' leigfeá 'un an aonaigh mé?
O mother will you let me go to the fair?

So we can outlive the sweet parents of the pearl,
the grain, the wood-grain embellished by oil.

Meet me, meet me, she begs. The brush
catches fire in the sunset. Unnoticed,
his fingers brush the hem of her linen skirt,
rest on the red seat leather.

How will I know when to meet you?
When only a breath is denser than air,
when petals swim in the colloid of fog,
when the witchhazel stirs with moonlight.
I don't know what it means to swim.
Which one is the witchhazel again?

When the milk cows walk
into the vertical chamber of dawn.
When the white bone grows from the thumb,
like a buck's horn, like a bit of broken glass.
When spring is still hushed and only the mud whistles.
When the laundry is dry or a little more than half-dry.

O mother will you let me lose track of time or remind me…
ah, my hands that were your hands…and now

Lawrenceville

it is disharmony that unifies   chalkdrawn skies, blackhaw
     with its fingers in the tar   brick wall

all rough surfaces   narrowing gloom
     man at the counter   sorting screws

his breath sweet from chaw
     blackpoll warblers   whipping   up the alley

so it comes to this   thinking
     what have I done what have I done   regret and then

the expunging cold   talking back   what's next?
     row-houses deliquescing   one by one

inside memory   of what an oven is
     you and your forgotten voice

afloat in summer clockvine
     because I have not heard you for so long

and right here I come and go and come   feeling the invisible
     from there nothing, nothing, and no one

Moss I

in the not-dead-moss
rusting-moss
sleeping-moss

slugabed eggs hidden
mussed head of winter wisteria
looks on, awaiting
rebirth of thousands

the stoplight head of the northern flicker
switches, switches,
aflight with suggestion
ovaries packed like pomegranates

there's trouble on my wedding finger
darkness soon to hatch
already releasing wingspan
mass-shooting on the news

already trembling organ
of the tongue, this time bit,
seduced, lie it there a little longer

means nothing
means it will get better won't it?

means legion starkling thoughts
all icy flight, all implanted

Moss II

i.

each hook
a set variation in small space
green halos bleached
to the root   mute
Archimedes' Screw measures
nothing but obedience to laws
chooses nothing but collared shirts
of the Mormon boys at dusk
witnessing   standing by the gate
under candy-pink crabapple

ii.

moss-mouthed words
that *atheist* nightshade, aphelion white folds
gowning dirtarms
the erect made more sublime
the erect enclosed
as marigolds between us
how much matters?
sunlight honey on the pavement
monkshood bodies
remembering maps, legends,
maps, legends

iii.

and the dead in us, dark-heeled bells wrung-out
rinsed curtains on the line
crows rising from the just-sown wheat
suggest last laugh's for the firemen
striving from ash to clear
unlike the rest of us
all water/sun direct and dumb
we run   looking for signs
in the pancakes

iv.

dioicous life, spores and gametophores
sphagnum drying on the rocks/trunks
trundled rock ear mushrooms
hell in the air
wars we can't get near
I mean, same as always, wish you were here

v.

dogwood blooms a big myth
snow grows first, biggest
all the other absent bodies
turn and turn over
like a tired engine
o battery let this be
how we are in relation to the past
new patterns of sound
in the past are whistles
and curled forks of green/gray
water and fog
at once generating the other
each each

Free Verse Editions

Edited by Jon Thompson

13 ways of happily by Emily Carr
Between the Twilight and the Sky by Jennie Neighbors
Blood Orbits by Ger Killeen
The Bodies by Chris Sindt
The Book of Isaac by Aidan Semmens
Canticle of the Night Path by Jennifer Atkinson
Child in the Road by Cindy Savett
Condominium of the Flesh by Valerio Magrelli, trans. by Clarissa Botsford
Contrapuntal by Christopher Kondrich
Country Album by James Capozzi
The Curiosities by Brittany Perham
Current by Lisa Fishman
Dismantling the Angel by Eric Pankey
Divination Machine by F. Daniel Rzicznek
Erros by Morgan Lucas Schuldt
Fifteen Seconds without Sorrow by Shim Bo-Seon, translated by Chung
    Eun-Gwi and Brother Anthony of Taizé
The Forever Notes by Ethel Rackin
The Flying House by Dawn-Michelle Baude
Go On by Ethel Rackin
Instances: Selected Poems by Jeongrye Choi, translated by Brenda Hillman,
    Wayne de Fremery, & Jeongrye Choi
The Magnetic Brackets by Jesús Losada, translated by Michael Smith &
    Luis Ingelmo
Man Praying by Donald Platt
A Map of Faring by Peter Riley
No Shape Bends the River So Long by Monica Berlin & Beth Marzoni
Overyellow, by Nicolas Pesquès, translated by Cole Swensen
Physis by Nicolas Pesque, translated by Cole Swensen
Pilgrimage Suites by Derek Gromadzki
Pilgrimly by Siobhán Scarry
Poems from above the Hill & Selected Work by Ashur Etwebi, translated by
    Brenda Hillman & Diallah Haidar
The Prison Poems by Miguel Hernández, translated by Michael Smith
Puppet Wardrobe by Daniel Tiffany
Quarry by Carolyn Guinzio

remanence by Boyer Rickel
Signs Following by Ger Killeen
Split the Crow by Sarah Sousa
Spine by Carolyn Guinzio
Spool by Matthew Cooperman
Summoned by Guillevic, translated by Monique Chefdor & Stella Harvey
Sunshine Wound by L. S. Klatt
System and Population, by Christopher Sindt
These Beautiful Limits by Thomas Lisk
They Who Saw the Deep by Geraldine Monk
The Thinking Eye by Jennifer Atkinson
This History That Just Happened by Hannah Craig
An Unchanging Blue: Selected Poems 1962–1975 by Rolf Dieter
    Brinkmann, translated by Mark Terrill
Under the Quick by Molly Bendall
Verge by Morgan Lucas Schuldt
The Wash by Adam Clay
We'll See by Georges Godeau, translated by Kathleen McGookey
What Stillness Illuminated by Yermiyahu Ahron Taub
Winter Journey [Viaggio d'inverno] by Attilio Bertolucci, translated by
    Nicholas Benson
Wonder Rooms by Allison Funk

About the Author

Hannah Craig is an Indiana native and a graduate of the University of Chicago. She won the 2016 Mississippi Review Prize and her manuscript was a finalist for the Akron Poetry Prize, the Fineline Competition, and the Autumn House Poetry Prize. Her work has appeared widely in such publications as *Smartish Pace, North American Review, Fence, Mississippi Review,* and *Prairie Schooner.* She lives in Pittsburgh, Pennsylvania.

Photograph of the author.

www.ingramcontent.com/pod-product-compliance
Lightning Source LLC
Chambersburg PA
CBHW022038090426
42741CB00007B/1120